W9-CHH-495

Presented to:

_____

From:

_____

Date:

_____

Christmas Is . . .

Honor Books

Christmas Is . . .
ISBN 1-56292-907-0
Copyright © 2000 by Honor Books

Introduction

*C*hristmas is many things to many people. We've picked just a few of the things that Christmas is to us and selected quotes, stories, Scriptures, songs, and even recipes to help inspire you and remind you that:

Christmas is giving—God's gift to us, His Son, Jesus Christ, inspires us to give to others.

Christmas is music—What would Christmas be without all those wonderful songs that remind us of His birth and life?

Christmas is cookies—Here's where the recipes come in. Christmas just isn't Christmas without a plateful of yummy cookies!

Christmas is tradition—mistletoe, Christmas cards, lights on the tree, and brightly wrapped packages. You'll find the origin of these wonderful Christmas customs, plus many more, as you read about the traditions of other countries.

Christmas is children—The wonder and mystery of Christmas is never lost on children. During this joyous season, approach Christmas with a childlike heart.

Christmas is hope—Christmas is the birthday of hope . . . the hope of all the world, our Savior, Jesus Christ.

Christmas is love—"God so loved the world that He gave . . . " and that love grows in our hearts and should overflow to others, especially during the Christmas season.

Christmas is joy—Joy to the world! There would be no joy in the earth without the baby born in Bethlehem.

Christmas is peace—"Peace on earth, good will to men," the angels announced at Jesus' birth. He is the one true source for peace on earth.

Christmas is Jesus—After all, He is the "reason for the season."

Have a blessed Christmas season and remember all the wonderful things that Christmas is!

Contents

Christmas Is Giving

Giving yourself is the greatest gift of all.

*Be imitators of God, therefore, as dearly loved
children and live a life of love, just as Christ
loved us and gave himself up for us.*

EPHESIANS 5:1-2

The African boy listened carefully as the teacher explained why people give presents to each other on Christmas Day. "The gift is an expression of our joy over the birth of Jesus and our friendship with each other," she said.

When Christmas Day came, the boy brought the teacher a seashell of lustrous beauty. "Where did you ever find such a beautiful shell?" the teacher exclaimed. The youth named the spot—a bay several miles away. The teacher was touched. "Why . . . why, it's gorgeous . . . wonderful, but you shouldn't have gone all that way to get a gift for me."

His eyes brightening, the boy answered, "Long walk part of gift."

—Gerald Horton Bath

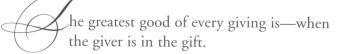

he greatest good of every giving is—when the giver is in the gift.

—George MacDonald

*Every good and perfect gift is from
above, coming down from the
Father of the heavenly lights.*

JAMES 1:17

This is Christmas—the real meaning of it.
God loving, searching, giving Himself—to us.

Man's needing, receiving, giving himself—to God.
Redemption's glorious exchange of gifts!

Without which we cannot live;
Without which we cannot give to those we love
   anything of lasting value.

This is the meaning of Christmas—
   the wonder and the glory of it.

—Ruth Bell Graham

I always like the gifts I get, but how I love the gifts I give!

—Carolyn Wells

For all things come from You, and from Your hand we have given You.

1 CHRONICLES 29:14 NASB

A pastor asked the church youth group to help a single mother who needed a car but could not afford one. He had found an inexpensive vehicle in good condition, and the youth group was to raise the funds to purchase it. They had numerous bake sales, car washes, and spaghetti dinners to raise money.

On Christmas Eve, the single mother, who knew nothing of these efforts, answered her doorbell and found the entire youth group standing at her door. The young people sang, "We Wish You a Merry Christmas," and one teen handed her the keys. Then the young people opened a path before her, and her eyes fell on the car she so desperately needed.

Years later, the young people still count that experience among the most memorable of all their teenage activities. One young man said, "It was one time we really did something important for Christ for Christmas. I'll never forget it."

—Gayle Edwards

hat can I give Him,

Poor as I am?

If I were a shepherd,

I would bring a lamb,

If I were a Wise Man

I would do my part—

Yet what I can I give Him,

Give my heart.

—Christina Georgina Rossetti

One recent Christmas I was visiting my parents, who live in a mining community in West Virginia. Times were bad. I noticed in front of me a young couple stopped near a lame man. The husband, obviously a miner, and his wife were talking in half whispers. The young husband looked down at his wife. Slowly, a smile came over his face and he agreed. She pulled out an old black change purse. Then she walked slowly to the lame man and turned the purse upside down. Coins rattled noisily into the old man's cup. "I'm wishin' you a merry Christmas," she whispered. Gratefully, the lame man reached out to shake her hand.

I watched them walk down the street. They were broke and would have to walk home. But I could tell by the bounce in their steps that it would not be a long walk. When they lightened their purse, they also lightened their hearts.

—Loren Young

Christmas is a time to remember the gift of God's giving nature in every area of life. He gave us the earth on which to live; fellow humans to love and with whom we can work and share; and great meaning in life—to serve others. The gift of God's Son, Jesus, gives us peace to enjoy all these other gifts as His family on earth—and to live in eternal joy. Merry Christmas to us who have received all God's gifts. Joy to the world!

The Most Important Things You Can Give on Christmas

Your time—Volunteer to help those less fortunate.

Your love—It's the thought that counts.

Your life—Jesus was born that you might be saved.

Your Lord—Share Jesus with your friends and family.

Do give books—religious or otherwise—for Christmas. They're never fattening, seldom sinful, and permanently personal.

—Lenora Hershey

Give, and it will be given to you. A good measure,
pressed down, shaken together and running over,
will be poured into your lap. For with the measure
you use, it will be measured to you.

LUKE 6:38

Christmas Is Music

Away in a Manger

Away in a manger, no crib for a bed,
The little Lord Jesus, laid down His sweet head;
The stars in the sky looked down where He lay,
The little Lord Jesus, asleep on the hay.

The cattle are lowing; the Baby awakes,
But little Lord Jesus, no crying He makes;

I love Thee, Lord Jesus! Look down from the sky,
And stay by my cradle till morning is nigh.

Be near me, Lord Jesus, I ask Thee to stay
Close by me forever, and love me, I pray;
Bless all the dear children in Thy tender care,
And fit us for heaven, to live with Thee there.

—Attributed to Martin Luther

The First Noel

The first noel the angel did say
Was to certain poor shepherds in fields as they lay;
In fields where they lay keeping their sheep
On a cold winter's night that was so deep.

They looked up and saw a star
Shining in the east, beyond them far;
And to the earth, it gave great light,
And so it continued both day and night.

And by the light of that same star,
Three wise men came from country far;
To seek for a king was their intent,
And to follow the star wherever it went.

Then entered in those wise men three;
Fall reverently upon their knee,
And offered there, in His presence,
Their gold and myrrh and frankincense.

Then let us all with one accord
Sing praises to our heavenly Lord,
That hath made heaven and earth of naught,
And with His blood mankind hath bought.

Noel, noel! Noel, noel!
Born is the King of Israel.

Emmanuel

O come, O come, Emmanuel,
And ransom captive Israel,
That mourns in lonely exile here
Until the Son of God appear.

O come, Thou Dayspring, come and cheer
Our spirits by Thine advent here;

O drive away the shades of night
And pierce the clouds and bring us light.

Rejoice!
Rejoice!
Emmanuel shall come to thee,
O Israel.

Hark! The Herald Angels Sing

Hark! The herald angels sing, "Glory to the newborn King;
Peace on earth, and mercy mild—God and sinners reconciled!"
Joyful, all ye nations rise, join the triumph of the skies;
With angelic hosts proclaim, "Christ is born in Bethlehem!"
Hark! The herald angels sing, "Glory to the newborn King!"

Christ, by highest heaven adored, Christ, the everlasting Lord!
Late in time behold Him come, offspring of a virgin's womb.

Veiled in flesh the Godhead see; hail the incarnate Deity,
Pleased as man with men to dwell, Jesus, our Emmanuel.
Hark! The herald angels sing, "Glory to the newborn King!"

Hail the heaven born Prince of Peace! Hail the Sun of
Righteousness! Light and life to all He brings, risen with healing
in His wings. Mild He lays His glory by, born that man no more
may die, Born to raise the sons of earth. Born to give them
second birth.

Hark! The herald angels sing, "Glory to the newborn King!"

—John Wesley

What Child Is This?

What child is this, who, laid to rest,
on Mary's lap is sleeping?
Whom angels greet with anthems sweet,
while shepherds watch are keeping?

This, this is Christ, the King,
whom shepherds guard and angels sing;
Haste, haste to bring Him laud—
the Babe, the Son of Mary.

Why lies He in such mean estate
where ox and ass are feeding?
Good Christian, fear, for sinners here
the silent Word is pleading.

So bring Him incense, gold and myrrh—
come, peasant king, to own Him;
The King of kings salvation brings,
let loving hearts enthrone Him.

—William C. Dix

I Heard the Bells on Christmas Day

I heard the bells on Christmas day
Their old, familiar carols play,
And wild and sweet
The words repeat
Of peace on earth, goodwill to men.

I thought how, as the day had come,
The belfries of all Christendom
Had rolled along
Th' unbroken song
Of peace on earth, goodwill to men.

Then pealed the bells more loud and deep:
"God is not dead, nor doth He sleep;
The wrong shall fail,
The right prevail,
With peace on earth, goodwill to men."

Till, ringing, singing on its way,
The world revolved from night to day,
A voice, a chime,
A chant sublime
Of peace on earth, goodwill to men!

—Henry Wadsworth Longfellow

O Come, All Ye Faithful

O come, all ye faithful, joyful and triumphant;
O come ye, O come ye to Bethlehem;
Come and behold Him; born the King of angels!
Refrain: O come, let us adore Him, Christ the Lord.

Sing, choirs of angels, sing in exultation,
O sing, all ye bright hosts of heav'n above!
Glory to God, all glory in the highest!
Refrain: O come, let us adore Him, Christ the Lord.

Yea, Lord, we greet Thee, born this happy morning,
Jesus, to Thee be all glory giv'n;
Word of the Father, now in flesh appearing!
Refrain: O come, let us adore Him, Christ the Lord.

—Latin hymn, English translation by Frederick Oakley

Silent Night

Silent night! Holy night!
All is calm, all is bright
'Round yon virgin mother and Child,
Holy Infant, so tender and mild
Sleep in heavenly peace,
Sleep in heavenly peace.

Silent night! Holy night!
Shepherds quake at the sight;
Glories stream from heaven afar;
Heavenly hosts sing, "Alleluia!
Christ the Saviour is born,
Christ the Saviour is born."

Silent night! Holy night!
Son of God, love's pure light
Radiant beams from Thy holy face,
With the dawn of redeeming grace,
Jesus, Lord, at Thy birth,
Jesus, Lord, at Thy birth.

—Franz Gruber and Joseph Mohr

et's allow the joy of Christ's birth to be reflected on our faces and heard in our glad singing of praises to Him all through this Christmas season.

Sing to the LORD a new song; sing to the LORD,
all the earth. Sing to the LORD, praise his name;
proclaim his salvation day after day.

PSALM 96:1-2

Christmas Is Cookies

Christmas Eggnog Cookies

2¼ cups all-purpose flour
1 teaspoon baking powder
½ teaspoon ground nutmeg
½ teaspoon ground cinnamon
1½ sticks unsalted butter, softened to room temperature
1¼ cups sugar
1 teaspoon vanilla extract
2 large egg yolks
½ cup eggnog
   ground nutmeg

Preheat oven to 300°. Combine flour, baking powder, nutmeg, and cinnamon, and set aside. In a separate bowl, use a mixer to cream butter and sugar. Add vanilla, egg yolks, and eggnog. Beat on medium speed until mixture is smooth. Add the flour mixture and beat on low just until mixture is combined. Drop by teaspoonfuls, 1 inch apart, onto ungreased cookie sheets. Sprinkle with nutmeg. Bake for 20 to 22 minutes or until bottoms turn light brown. Place cookies on wire rack to cool.

Makes about 36 cookies.

Date Nut Dandies

2   eggs, beaten
1   cup sugar
1   stick butter
1   cup chopped dates
2½   cups crispy rice cereal
1   cup chopped nuts
     grated coconut

In a saucepan, combine eggs, sugar, butter, and dates. Bring to a rapid boil. Boil for 4 minutes, stirring constantly. Remove from heat; stir in cereal and nuts. Form into small balls. Roll in coconut. Place on waxed paper.

Makes about 40 cookies.

Christmas Curls

1   stick butter, softened to room temperature
½   cup sugar
1   teaspoon vanilla extract
2   egg whites
⅔   cup all-purpose flour

Preheat oven to 375°. In a large bowl, cream butter, sugar, and vanilla, with mixer on medium speed, until light and fluffy. Add egg whites and flour; blend well. Drop batter by the teaspoonful, 3 inches apart, onto an ungreased cookie sheet. With the back of a spoon, spread each cookie out to form 3-inch rounds. Bake for 5 minutes or until edges are light brown. Working with one cookie at a time, loosen from cookie sheet with a spatula and then quickly wrap tightly around the handle of a wooden spoon. Slide cookie off spoon and place each, seam side down, on a wire rack to cool.

Makes about 36 cookies.

Strawberry Crisps

1½ sticks butter, softened to room temperature
1 cup firmly packed light-brown sugar
1¾ cups all-purpose flour
½ teaspoon salt
½ teaspoon baking soda
1½ cups quick-cooking rolled oats
1 18-ounce jar strawberry jam

Preheat oven to 400°. In a large bowl, cream butter and brown sugar, with mixer set on medium speed, until smooth. Stir together dry ingredients. Gradually add dry ingredients to creamed mixture; mix until crumbly. Press ½ of the mixture into a greased 13 x 9-inch baking pan. Spread with jam. Sprinkle remaining crumb mixture over the top and press lightly into jam. Bake for 18 to 20 minutes or until lightly browned. Cool for 5 minutes before cutting into squares.

Makes 24 cookies.

Lemon Twists

1⅓ sticks butter
¾ cup sugar
1 egg, beaten
1½ cups self-rising flour
¼ cup ground almonds
1 teaspoon grated lemon rind

Preheat oven to 400°. In a large bowl, cream butter and sugar, with mixer set on medium speed, until light and fluffy. Stir in egg. Slowly add flour, almonds, and lemon rind. Mix until well blended. Roll pieces of dough into 4-inch ropes. Twist into "S" shapes on a greased cookie sheet. Bake for about 10 minutes or until golden. Use spatula to place cookies on wire rack to cool. Store in airtight container.

Makes about 48 cookies.

Melting Moments

1   cup all-purpose flour
2   tablespoons cornstarch
½   cup confectioners' sugar
2   sticks butter, softened to room temperature
1½ cups coconut

Preheat oven to 300°. In a large bowl, combine flour, cornstarch, and sugar. Cream in butter, with mixer set on medium speed, until soft dough forms. Form into ¾-inch balls. Roll in coconut. Place 1½ inches apart on an ungreased cookie sheet. Bake for 20 to 25 minutes, or until lightly browned.

Makes about 30 cookies.

Chocolate Praline Cookies

1   stick plus 3 tablespoons butter
2   cups firmly packed brown sugar
2   eggs
1   teaspoon vanilla extract
1½ cups all-purpose flour
¼   teaspoon salt
2   teaspoons baking powder
½   cup chopped nuts
1   12-ounce package semisweet chocolate chips

Preheat oven to 350°. In a large saucepan, melt butter. Remove from heat and stir in sugar, eggs, and vanilla. Blend in the next 3 ingredients. Add nuts and chocolate chips. Place in greased 11 x 9-inch pan. Bake for 35 minutes. When cool, cut into squares.

Makes about 18 cookies.

Winter Wonderland Bars

1	stick butter
1	cup graham cracker crumbs
1	6-ounce package semisweet chocolate chips
1	6-ounce package butterscotch chips
1	cup shredded coconut
1	cup chopped nuts
1	15-ounce can sweetened condensed milk

Preheat oven to 350°. Melt butter in a 9 x 11-inch pan. Layer remaining ingredients, in order given, in buttered pan. Bake for 25 minutes. Cool in pan and cut into bars.

Makes 30 bars.

Wafer Ribbons

½   stick butter, softened to room temperature
2   squares chocolate, melted
1   teaspoon salt
1   cup all-purpose flour
1   cup confectioners' sugar
¼   cup milk
1   teaspoon vanilla extract
½   cup chopped pecans

Preheat oven to 325°. In a large bowl, cream butter, with mixer set on medium speed, until light. Blend in melted chocolate. Sift next 3 ingredients together and add to creamed mixture. Blend in milk and vanilla; mix well. Stir in nuts. Spread thinly into a greased 11 x 17-inch pan. Bake for 20 minutes. Cut into squares when cool.

Makes about 36 cookies.

Christmas Trees

- 2 sticks butter, softened to room temperature
- 1 3-ounce package cream cheese, softened to room temperature
- ½ cup sugar
- 1 teaspoon vanilla extract
- 2 cups all-purpose flour, sifted
  green decorating sugar

Preheat oven to 375°. In large bowl, cream butter, cream cheese, and sugar, with mixer set on medium speed; blend in vanilla. Mix in flour a little at a time. Fill cookie press, using tree plate attachment. Press cookies onto an ungreased cookie sheet. Decorate as desired. Bake for 6 to 7 minutes or until lightly golden. Use spatula to place cookies on wire rack to cool.

Makes about 24 cookies.

Heavenly Vanilla Spritz

2   sticks butter, softened to room temperature
½   cup sugar
1   egg, beaten
½   teaspoon vanilla extract
2¼   cups all-purpose flour
     decorating sugar

Preheat oven to 350°. In a mixing bowl, cream butter and sugar, with mixer set on medium speed, until light and fluffy. Blend in egg and vanilla. Gradually mix in flour, a little at a time, until well blended. Fill a cookie press with dough. Using a star or bar attachment, press cookies onto an ungreased cookie sheet. Sprinkle with decorating sugar. Bake for 8 to 10 minutes or until lightly golden. Use spatula to place cookies on wire rack to cool.

Makes about 60 to 70 cookies.

Christmas Tea Cookies

1   stick butter, softened to room temperature
1   cup sugar
2   cups all-purpose flour
¼   teaspoon salt
1   teaspoon baking powder
2   eggs
½   teaspoon vanilla extract

Preheat oven to 350°. In a large bowl, cream butter and sugar, with mixer set on medium speed, until light and fluffy. Sift next 3 ingredients together. Add to creamed mixture, alternately with eggs and vanilla; mix well. Roll on floured surface to a ⅛-inch thickness. Cut into desired shapes. Place on lightly greased and floured cookie sheet. Bake for 8 to 10 minutes or until lightly golden. Use spatula to place cookies on wire rack to cool.

Makes 60 cookies.

Cheery Oatmeal Macaroons

1   egg white
¼   teaspoon salt
1   cup sugar
¼   cup grated coconut
1   cup regular or quick-cooking rolled oats
½   teaspoon vanilla extract

Preheat oven to 350°. In a large bowl, combine egg white and salt; beat, with mixer set on low speed, until foamy. Gradually add sugar, beating at medium speed until stiff peaks form. Fold in remaining ingredients. Drop batter by the teaspoonful onto a greased and floured cookie sheet. Bake for 10 to 12 minutes or until golden brown. Use spatula to place cookies on wire rack to cool.

Makes about 24 cookies.

Christmas Is Tradition

The practice of singing Christmas carols appears to be almost as old as the celebration of the day itself. In the first days of the church, the bishops sang carols on Christmas Day, recalling the songs sung by the angels at the birth of Christ.

Praise him for his majestic glory,
the glory of his name.

PSALM 29:2 TLB

In Italy, the *Presepio* or *crib* is as characteristic of Christmas as the tree is in Germany.

Every home, even the poorest, has a *Presepio* of some kind, and the churches have very elaborate ones. The people place humble gifts of nuts and apples in the hands of the life-sized figures.

Whatever measure you use to give—large or small—will be used to measure what is given back to you.

LUKE 6:38 TLB

According to tradition, mistletoe, when used at Christmas, has romantic significance.

A spray is cunningly hung over a doorway or place of vantage beneath which the romantic "mistletoe kiss" may be claimed. A berry is plucked after each kiss. When the berries are gone, the privilege of kissing ceases.

Greet one another with a holy kiss.

ROMANS 16:16 NKJV

The first real Christmas cards appear to have been printed in London in 1846. Almost one thousand copies were made—that would have been considered a very large sale at the time.

It was not until about 1860 that the custom of using cards to convey Christmas greetings became popular. The tradition has gained strength through the years, and today, Christmas cards are produced by the millions.

Now here is my greeting which I am writing with my own hand. . . . May the blessing of our Lord Jesus Christ be upon you all.

2 THESSALONIANS 3:17-18 TLB

A Christmas candle is
a lovely thing:
It makes no noise at all,
But softly gives itself away;
While quite unselfish, it grows small.

—Eva K. Logue

The spirit of man is the candle of the LORD,
searching all the inward parts.

PROVERBS 20:27 KJV

CHRISTMAS IS ...

In the early 1900s a young Denver boy who was sick asked his father to put lights on the big evergreen just outside his window. The boy's father, who operated an electrical business, strung colored lights on the evergreen. His son watched them sparkle like emeralds and rubies against their ermine mantle of snow.

In horse-drawn carriages and chugging automobiles, people came for miles around to admire the tree. The next year, neighbors joined in the outdoor tree-trimming.

It wasn't long before the lighted Christmas trees spread from home to home and became a holiday tradition. Today, in city parks, along highways, on dark and snow-drifted lawns alike, lighted living trees remind millions of the birth of Christ.

—Grady Johnson

*I*n medieval times, the bells were tolled for one hour before midnight on Christmas Eve.

The purpose of the tolling, it was said, was to give the powers of darkness notice of the approaching birth of the Savior. In England, it was called, "Tolling the Devil's Knell" to signify the triumph of Christ's birth.

Praise the Lord, you angels of his; praise his glory and his strength.

PSALM 29:1 TLB

Xmas

*D*uring the holiday season, it has become commonplace to see an "X" replacing the word "Christ" in the word "Christmas." This is viewed by many as a crass attempt to separate the Savior from the season's festivities.

In fact, "X" is an abbreviation for "Christ." It originated from the Greek letter "X" *(chi),* beginning the name of Christ (the Anointed).

Those who love Christ can now find cause to rejoice even when urged to have a "Merry Xmas!"

> *The Spirit of the LORD is upon Me,*
> *because He has anointed Me.*
>
> *LUKE 4:18 NKJV*

61

Christmas plays and pageants are popular in Poland, where the Christmas story is recited in verse and acted out by marionettes. Polish boys in costumes go from house to house carrying Christmas cribs and singing carols.

It is a Polish custom not to serve Christmas dinner until the evening star has appeared. A vacant chair is always placed at the table to signify that a place has been made for the little child of Bethlehem.

*When they saw the star, they
rejoiced exceedingly with great joy.*

MATTHEW 2:10 NASB

touchingly beautiful Christmas custom is observed at early Mass on Christmas morning in some parts of South America. As the Nativity is reenacted, an Indian lullaby is sung to quiet the Christ child in His cradle of straw. The music of little bells and rattles can be heard as worshippers celebrate the divine birth.

I will lie down in peace and sleep, for though
I am alone, O Lord, you will keep me safe.

PSALM 4:8 TLB

In Egypt, Christians burn candles, lamps, and logs in great numbers on Christmas Eve as symbols of the "shepherds' fire."

*For You will light my lamp; the LORD
my God will enlighten my darkness.*

PSALM 18:28 NKJV

*W*ell-to-do families in Serbia keep open house for three days at Christmas, and all visitors, friends or enemies, strangers or beggars, are welcome to come to the table.

On Christmas Eve, the Serbians have a saying: "Tonight earth is blended with Paradise."

> *When you put on a dinner . . . invite the poor,*
> *the crippled, the lame, and the blind . . . God will*
> *reward you for inviting those who can't repay you.*
>
> LUKE 14:12-14 TLB

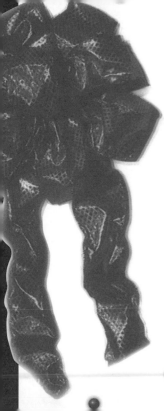

*E*ight things are usually associated with Christmas.

First and foremost is its religious significance as the birthday of Christ. The other seven are: hanging the mistletoe, burning the Yule log, the Christmas tree, the Christmas carol, the greeting card, the Christmas stocking, and Santa Claus.

These eight have remained symbols of Christmas throughout the years.

Jesus Christ is the same
yesterday, today, and forever.

HEBREWS 13:8 TLB

Christmas Is Children

You can never truly enjoy Christmas until you can look up into the Father's face and tell Him you have received His Christmas gift.

—John R. Rice

If you . . . know how to give good gifts to your children, how much more will your Father in heaven give good gifts to those who ask him!

MATTHEW 7:11

The way to Christmas lies through an ancient gate. . . . It is a little gate, child-high, child-wide, and there is a password: "Peace on earth to men of good will." May you, this Christmas, become as a little child again and enter into His kingdom.

—Angelo Patri

*C*HRISTMAS IS ...

*W*hatever else you give to your children, give them roots and give them wings.

> *Every year his parents went to Jerusalem for the*
> *Feast of the Passover. When he was twelve years old,*
> *they went up to the Feast, according to the custom.*
>
> *LUKE 2:41-42*

*T*he children could hardly wait to open presents. But wait they would. For every Christmas morning, their father shared a unique present that required them to take a family drive.

A friend of his had discovered and purchased a tract of land in the middle of the desert area they lived in. It had several natural springs that accented a rare desert wetland. He had turned it into a bird refuge. The family visited just once a year, always on Christmas.

"Some things are so special that, if you did them every day, you'd ruin them for sure," the father would say as the family huddled close to celebrate a tradition that became a cherished memory.[1]

—Jennifer Gillia Costa

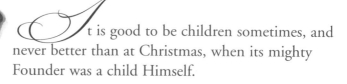

It is good to be children sometimes, and never better than at Christmas, when its mighty Founder was a child Himself.

—Charles Dickens

And a little child will lead them.

ISAIAH 11:6

Jam Session

One Sunday evening, I overheard my five-year-old, Julie, practicing "Hark the Herald Angels Sing," a song she'd been rehearsing that morning in church for next week's Christmas program.

It was all I could do to suppress my laughter when, in place of "with the angelic host proclaim," Julie sang, "with the jelly toast proclaim."[2]

—Marilyn Clark

The Lamb

Little lamb, who made thee?
Dost thou know who made thee,
Gave thee life and bade thee feed
By the stream and o'er the mead;

Gave thee clothing of delight,
Softest clothing, woolly, bright;
Gave thee such a tender voice,
Making all the vales rejoice?

Little lamb, who made thee?
Dost thou know who made thee?
Little lamb, I'll tell thee;
Little lamb, I'll tell thee.

He is called by thy name,
For He calls Himself a Lamb;
He is meek and He is mild,
He became a little child.

I a child and thou a lamb,
We are called by His name.
Little lamb, God bless thee!
Little lamb, God bless thee!

—William Blake

None will ever find a way
To banish Christ from Christmas Day . . .
For with each child there's born again
A mystery that baffles men.

—Helen Steiner Rice

"Forgive Us Our Christmases"

The story has been published of a little girl caught in the pre-Christmas swirl of activity, all of which seemed to be coming to a head on Christmas Eve. Dad, loaded down with bundles, seemed to have an even greater number of worries. Mom, under the pressure of getting ready for the great occasion, had yielded to tears several times during the day. The little girl found that she was always underfoot, and sometimes adult kindness to her wore thin.

Finally, near tears herself, she was hustled off to bed. There, kneeling to pray the Lord's Prayer before finally tumbling in, her mind and tongue betrayed her, and she prayed, "Forgive us our Christmases as we forgive those who Christmas against us."

Too often we leave out the Christ of Christmas. Too often He is crowded out of our busy lives. Remember, the best gift won't be found in a box but in a person.[3]

—Unknown

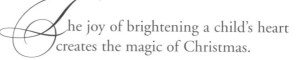

The joy of brightening a child's heart
creates the magic of Christmas.

—W. C. Jones

*Whatever you did for one of the least
of these brothers of mine, you did for me.*

MATTHEW 25:40

78

Two boys couldn't wait for Christmas. They'd asked for trains, and there were hints they'd get them. On Christmas morning, they were up before dawn.

Sure enough, under the tree sat a gleaming passenger train for the younger boy and a sturdy freight train for the older boy. They ran excitedly into their parents' bedroom, their eyes sparkling with delight. Mom said they were great. Dad showed honest but groggy interest. Another surprise stood in the basement: a huge table covered with track, wired so they could run both trains at the same time. They loved it!

The boys didn't know their dad had worked all night building, laying track, and wiring. They couldn't appreciate his hours of planning, expensive shopping, and lost sleep. But years later they would understand their father's sacrificial love when they, too, became fathers. What loving father's heart doesn't leap for joy at blessing his children?

—Robert Murphy

Oh, come little children from cot and hall,
Oh, come to the manger, in Bethlehem's stall,
There meekly He lieth, the heavenly Child,
So poor and so humble, so sweet and so mild.

—Unknown

*Bethlehem . . . out of you will come a ruler
who will be the shepherd of my people Israel.*

MATTHEW 2:6

Christmas Is Hope

In a world that seems not only to be changing, but even to be dissolving, there are some tens of millions of us who want Christmas to be the same . . . with the same old greeting "Merry Christmas" and no other.

We long for the abiding love among men of goodwill which the season brings . . . believing in this ancient miracle of Christmas with its softening, sweetening influence to tug at our heartstrings once again.

We want to hold on to the old customs and traditions because they strengthen our family ties, bind us to our friends, make us one with all mankind for whom the child was born, and bring us back again to the God who gave His only begotten Son, that "whosoever believeth in Him should not perish, but have everlasting life."

So we will not "spend" Christmas . . . nor "observe" Christmas.

We will "keep" Christmas—keep it as it is . . . in all the loveliness of its ancient traditions.

May we keep it in our hearts, that we may be kept in its hope.

—Peter Marshall

ake Christ out of Christmas, and December becomes the bleakest and most colorless month of the year.

Today in the town of David a Savior has been born to you; he is Christ the Lord.

LUKE 2:11

CHRISTMAS IS . . .

This old, sobbing world of ours is one year older than it was when the last Christmas carol was chanted. It had another twelve months of experiments and experiences; of advancement on many lines of human research, scientific discovery, and acquisition. But it has not outgrown Jesus Christ. For Him it has discovered no substitute. The Star of Bethlehem is the only star that never sets.

—T. L. Cuyler

Of the increase of His government and peace there will be no end.

ISAIAH 9:7 NKJV

Although the world is full of suffering, it is full also of the overcoming of it.

—Helen Keller

Comfort ye my people.

ISAIAH 40:1 KJV

*R*ise, happy morn, rise, holy morn,
Draw forth the cheerful day from night;
O Father, touch the East, and light
The light that shone when Hope was born.

—Alfred, Lord Tennyson

The Light from heaven came into the world.

JOHN 3:19 TLB

*W*e may see God by our
intellect, but we only can
find him with our heart.

—Cotvos

No one has ever seen God. It is God the
only Son, who is close to the Father's heart,
who has made him known.

JOHN 1:18 NRSV

Almost nobody has seen God, and almost nobody has any real idea of what He is like.

The truth is, the idea of seeing God suddenly and standing in a very bright light is not necessarily a completely comforting and appealing idea.

But everyone has seen babies, and most people like them. If God wanted to be loved as well as feared, he moved correctly here.

Christmas is either all falsehood or it is the truest thing in the world.[4]

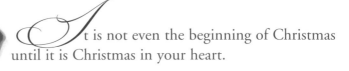

It is not even the beginning of Christmas until it is Christmas in your heart.

—Richard Roberts

Hope does not disappoint us, because
God has poured out his love into
our hearts by the Holy Spirit,
whom he has given us.

ROMANS 5:5

When the song of the angels is stilled,
When the star in the sky is gone,
When the kings and princes are home,
When the shepherds are back with their flock,

Then the work of Christmas begins:

To find the lost, to heal the broken;
To feed the hungry, to release the prisoner;
To rebuild the nations, to bring peace among enemies;
To make music in your heart.[5]

—Howard Thurman

Christmas is not a time or a season but a state of mind. To cherish peace and goodwill, to be plenteous in mercy, is to have the real spirit of Christmas. If we think on these things, there will be born in us a Savior and over us all will shine a star, sending its gleam of hope to the world.

—Calvin Coolidge

When God wants
an important thing done in this world,
or a wrong righted,
He goes about it in a very singular way.

God does not release thunderbolts
or stir up an earthquake.

God simply has a tiny, helpless baby born,
perhaps in an obscure home,
perhaps of very humble parents.

Then He puts the idea into the parents' hearts,
they put it into the baby's mind,
and then—God waits.

—Edward T. Sullivan

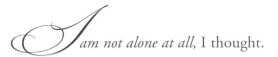

am not alone at all, I thought.

I was never alone at all.

And that, of course, is the message of Christmas.

We are never alone.

Not when the night is darkest, the wind coldest, the world seemingly most indifferent.

For this is still the time God chooses.

—Taylor Caldwell

Christmas Is Love

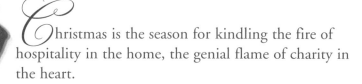

Christmas is the season for kindling the fire of hospitality in the home, the genial flame of charity in the heart.

—Washington Irving

And now these three remain: faith, hope and love.
But the greatest of these is love.

1 CORINTHIANS 13:13

I have always thought of Christmas . . .
as a good time:
a kind, forgiving, charitable, pleasant time;
the only time I know of, in the long calendar of the year,
when men and women seem by one consent
to open their shut-up hearts freely. . . .

And though it has never put
a scrap of gold or silver in my pocket,
I believe that it has done me good,
and will do me good.

And so, as Tiny Tim said,
"A merry Christmas to us all;
God bless us, every one!"

—Charles Dickens

he means to gain happiness is to throw out from oneself, like a spider, in all directions an adhesive web of love, and to catch in it all that comes.

—Leo Tolstoy

Love your neighbor as yourself.

MARK 12:31

*S*ometimes Sarah hated Christmas. "Why do you let those strangers come here for dinner?" she whined to her mother. "They should eat at their own house!"

Sarah's mother hugged her daughter. "Let's go for a drive while the turkey cooks." In the car, they sang Christmas carols until they came to an area Sarah had never seen before.

"Why is that man sleeping on the sidewalk?" Sarah asked.

"This is where some people live," her mother replied.

"Outside? But it's cold!" Sarah looked down at her own warm coat and shoes. Her stomach growled, and she thought about Christmas dinner. "Are they hungry, too?" Her mother nodded.

At dinner, Sarah hugged every "stranger" and presented a gift. Wrapped in pretty Christmas paper was every sheet, towel, blanket, shoe, hat, and mitten Sarah could find in the house.

—Gayle Edwards

*L*ove is that condition in which the happiness of another person is essential to your own.

—Robert Heinlein

But God showed his great love for us by sending Christ to die for us while we were still sinners.

ROMANS 5:8 TLB

One Christmas Day, five-year-old Amy unwrapped a beautiful doll given to her by her grandmother.

"Oh, thank you, Grandma!" Amy squealed excitedly, hugging her new gift. Amy played with her new doll for several hours, but toward the end of the day, she brought out one of her old dolls. She cradled the tattered doll in her arms. It had lost much of its hair; its nose was broken; one eye was gone.

"Well, well," smiled Grandma. "I see you like this doll the best."

"I like the beautiful doll you gave me, Grandma," replied Amy.

"But I love this old doll the most, because if I didn't love her, no one else would."[6]

—Glenn Van Ekeren

Christmas, my child, is love in action. Every time we love, every time we give, it's Christmas.

—Dale Evans Rogers

As the Father has loved me, so have I loved you. Now remain in my love. If you obey my commands, you will remain in my love, just as I have obeyed my Father's commands and remain in his love.

JOHN 15:9-10

It ain't the gift a feller gits, it ain't the shape ner size,
that sets the heart to beatin' and puts sunshine in yer eyes.
It ain't the value of the thing, ner how it's wrapped ner tied;
it's something else aside from this that makes you glad inside.
It's knowin' that it represents a love both deep an' true,
that someone carries in his heart and wants to slip to you.
It's knowin' that some folks love you and tell you in this way—
jest sorter actin' out the things they long to say.
So 'tain't the gift a feller gets, ner how it's wrapped ner tied,
it's knowin' that folks like you, that makes you glad inside.

*So in everything, do to others what you
would have them do to you.*

MATTHEW 7:12

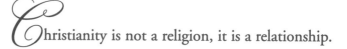

Christianity is not a religion, it is a relationship.

—Dr. Thieme

For God so loved the world that he gave his one and only Son, that whoever believes in him shall not perish but have eternal life.

JOHN 3:16

Christmas Time

Christmas time is here once again
Snow is falling softly again
It's the time of year
When everyone belongs together
Never mind the cold or the weather
Take a chance, share some love
Christmas time is here once again
People stop to talk with a friend
Say a kindly word
And everything seems so much better
Little things, they don't seem to matter
Take a chance, share some love

—Grace Lucas

The best Christmas gift of all is the presence of a happy family all wrapped up with one another.

*If we love one another, God abides in us,
and His love has been perfected in us.*

1 JOHN 4:12 NKJV

When Christmas Is Over

We've put away the ornaments,
And burned the Christmas tree;
The Christmas fun is over—but
The Christ Child, where is He?

He lives in gifts and toys we share
With children who have few
And in the acts of kindness
We do the whole year through.

—Corinna Marsh

I never realized God's birth before,
How He grew likest God in being born . . .
Such ever was love's way—to rise, it stoops.

—Robert Browning

*And Jesus grew in wisdom and stature,
and in favor with God and men.*

LUKE 2:52

*H*ere is love, that
God sent His Son,
His Son who never offended,
His Son who was always
His delight.

—John Bunyan

This is my Son, whom I love;
with him I am well pleased.

MATTHEW 3:17

Immense in mercy and with an incredible love,
[God] embraced us. He took our sin-dead lives
and made us alive in Christ.

EPHESIANS 2:4-5 THE MESSAGE

*L*oving Father, help us remember the birth of Jesus, that we may share in the song of the angels, the gladness of the shepherds, and the wisdom of the wise men.

Close the door of hate and open the door of love all over the world. Let kindness come with every gift and good desires with every greeting. Deliver us from evil by the blessing which Christ brings and teach us to be merry with clean hearts.

May the Christmas morning make us happy to be Your children and the Christmas evening bring us to our beds with grateful thoughts, forgiving and forgiven, for Jesus' sake.

Amen.

—Robert Louis Stevenson

It is Christmas every time you let God love others through you . . . every time you smile at your brother and offer him your hand.

—Mother Teresa

Freely you have received, freely give.

MATTHEW 10:8

Christmas Is Joy

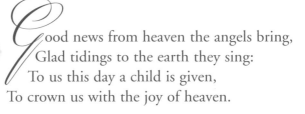

Good news from heaven the angels bring,
Glad tidings to the earth they sing:
To us this day a child is given,
To crown us with the joy of heaven.

—Martin Luther

This Good News was promised long ago by
God's prophets in the Old Testament.

ROMANS 1:2 TLB

*G*ood Christian men, rejoice
With heart, and soul, and voice;
Now ye hear of endless bliss: Joy! Joy!
Jesus Christ was born for this!
He hath opened the heav'nly door,
And man is blessed ever more.
Christ was born for this!
Christ was born for this!

—J. M. Neale

For unto us a Child is born, unto us a Son is given.

ISAIAH 9:6 NKJV

*J*oy is simply love looking at its treasures. A Christian's joy is in loving Christ and loving other people because Christ loves them; it is in doing good to others, and so having a Christmas perpetually.

—T. L. Cuyler

We love Him because He first loved us.

1 JOHN 4:19 NKJV

Somehow not only for Christmas
But all the long year through,
The joy that you give to others
Is the joy that comes back to you.
And the more you spend in blessing
The poor and lonely and sad,
The more of your heart's possessing
Returns to make you glad.

—John Greenleaf Whittier

*E*ternal life and endless joy
are parts of the gift.

You will fill me with joy in your presence.

PSALM 16:11

All you who have a troubled heart,
listen to the angel's song:
"I bring you tidings of great joy!"
Jesus did not come to condemn you.
If you want to define Christ rightly,
then pay heed to how the angel defines Him:
A great joy!

—Martin Luther

*L*aughter is the sweetest music that ever greeted the human ear.

> *Our mouths were filled with laughter, our tongues with songs of joy. Then it was said among the nations, "The LORD has done great things for them."*
>
> *PSALM 126:2*

Sing hey!
Sing hey!
For Christmas Day;
Twin mistletoe
And holly,
For friendship
Glows
In winter snows,
And so let's all
Be jolly.

—Unknown

Our first Christmas gift is the gift of gifts, Jesus Himself, the Son of God. Without Christ there is no Christmas, for a Christmas without Christ is meaningless.

But the tiny babe in the crib has conquered all hearts. His birthday has become a day of joy for the whole world.

It is not difficult to see, therefore, why events that fell on this birthday or happenings related to the sacred festival are of intense interest to every lover of the Christ child.

How can we explain the mysterious fascination that hovers over every Christmas season? Is it not that all men inherently sense that Jesus continues to shower the gifts of His grace on all humanity?

The antiphon of the "Magnificat" for the second vespers of Christmas Day best expresses the joy in our hearts:

"This day Christ is born; this day the Saviour hath appeared; this day the angels sing on earth, the archangels rejoice; this day the just exult, saying: Glory to God in the highest, alleluia."

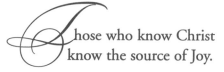hose who know Christ
know the source of Joy.

—Charles R. Hembree

Jesus Christ is the same
yesterday, today, and forever.

HEBREWS 13:8 TLB

Everywhere, everywhere Christmas tonight!
For the Christ child who comes is the master of all;
No palace too great—no cottage too small.

—Phillips Brooks

That at the name of Jesus every knee should bow,
of those in heaven, and of those on earth,
and of those under the earth.

PHILIPPIANS 2:10 NKJV

125

*J*oy to the world! The Lord is come:
  Let earth receive her King;
Let ev'ry heart prepare Him room
And heav'n and nature sing.

He rules the world with truth and grace,
And makes the nations prove
The glories of His righteousness,
And wonders of His love.

—Isaac Watts

I will praise you with great joy.

PSALM 63:5 TLB

Christmas Is Peace

O morning stars, together
Proclaim the holy birth,
And praises sing to God the King,
And peace to men on earth.

—Phillips Brooks

Let the heavens be glad, the earth rejoice.
. . . "It is the Lord who reigns."

1 CHRONICLES 16:31 TLB

On a winter night when the moon is low
The rabbits hop on the frozen snow.
The woodpecker sleeps in his hole in the tree
And fast asleep is the chickadee.
Twelve o'clock and the world is still
As the Christmas star comes over the hill.
The angels sing, and sing again:
"Peace on earth, goodwill to men."[7]

—Marion Edey

He brought peace on earth and wants to bring it also into your soul—that peace which the world cannot give. He is the One who would save His people from their sins.

—Corrie ten Boom

Peace I leave with you; my peace I give you.
I do not give to you as the world gives.

JOHN 14:27

This is the month, and this the happy morn,

Wherein the Son of Heaven's eternal King,

Of wedded maid and virgin mother born,

Our great redemption from above did bring;

For so the holy sages once did sing, that He our deadly
forfeit should release;

And with His Father work us a perpetual peace. . . .

—John Milton

Peace is our gift to each other.

—Elie Wiesel

And suddenly there was with the angel a multitude of the heavenly host, praising God and saying, "Glory to God in the highest heaven, and on earth peace among those whom he favors!"

LUKE 2:13-14 NRSV

For Christmas in 1948, President Harry S Truman gave each of his staff members a brown leather bookmark. It was embossed with his personal motto:

I would rather have peace in the world than be President.

Peace on earth among men of goodwill!

This is the blessed promise of Christmas. It is the perfect antidote for any fear or hysteria that may enter our lives.

—Unknown

And the peace of God, which passeth all understanding, shall keep your hearts and minds through Christ Jesus.

PHILIPPIANS 4:7 KJV

Tell me the story of Jesus,
    Write on my heart every word;
Tell me the story most precious,
Sweetest that ever was heard.
Tell how the angels, in chorus,
Sang as they welcomed His birth,
"Glory to God in the highest!
Peace and good tiding to earth."

—Fanny J. Crosby

Voices in the Mist

The time draws near the birth of Christ:
   The moon is hid; the night is still;
   The Christmas bells from hill to hill
Answer each other in the mist.
Four voices of four hamlets round,
From far and near, on mead and moor,

Swell out and fail, as if a door
Were shut between me and the sound:
Each voice four changes on the wind,
That now dilate, and now decrease,
Peace and goodwill, goodwill and peace,
Peace and goodwill, to all mankind.

—Alfred, Lord Tennyson

et's approach Christmas with an expectant
hush, rather than a last-minute rush.

> *The meek will inherit the*
> *land and enjoy great peace.*
>
> PSALM 37:11

138

Residents of the small village of Beit Sahour light candles at dusk on Christmas, announcing their determination to keep the eternal message of peace alive.

Just east of Bethlehem, this is believed to be the village of the shepherds who heard the heavenly message, "Peace on earth, good will among all."

In this troubled region of the world where strife dominates, the lighting of candles is a clear testimony that peace is only possible when we turn to the Babe in a Manger.[8]

—Fred Strickert

Christmas peace is God's; and he must give it himself, with his own hand, or we shall never get it. Go then to God himself. Thou art his child, as Christmas Day declares; be not afraid to go unto thy Father. Pray to him; tell him what thou wantest: say, "Father, I am not moderate, reasonable, forbearing. I fear I cannot keep Christmas aright for I have not a peaceful Christmas spirit in me; and I know that I shall never get it by thinking, and reading, and understanding; for it passes all that, and lies far away beyond it, does peace, in the very essence of thine undivided, unmoved, absolute, eternal Godhead, which no change nor decay of this created world, nor sin or folly of men or devils, can ever alter; but which abideth forever what it is, in perfect rest, and perfect power and perfect love. O Father, give me thy Christmas peace.

—Charles Kingsley

Christmas Is Jesus

When we receive Christ, we experience completely the gift that is Christmas. Then, for us, Christmas is truly always, for Jesus said, "Lo, I am with you always," . . . and Christmas is Jesus!

—Dale Evans Rogers

"The virgin will be with child and will give birth to a son, and they will call him Immanuel"—which means, "God with us."

MATTHEW 1:23

God with us. That's what Immanuel means. The prophet Isaiah foretold Jesus' birth and said He would be called Immanuel and Wonderful Counselor, Mighty God, Everlasting Father, Prince of Peace.

No longer would we walk through life alone with God watching us from a distance. Jesus' birth, life, death, and resurrection eliminated the barrier of sin and death and brought God to us—and us to God.

In our darkest hours, in our saddest moments, when fear and violence and loneliness seem to rule the planet, let us take comfort that we are not alone. Immanuel. God with us.

—Rose Gallion

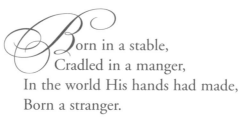

Born in a stable,
Cradled in a manger,
In the world His hands had made,
Born a stranger.

—Christina Georgina Rossetti

Before anything else existed,
there was Christ, with God.

JOHN 1:1 TLB

Some say that ever again
that season comes
wherein our Saviour's birth is celebrated
the bird of dawning
singeth all night long.

And then, they say,
no spirit dare stir abroad.
No planet strikes.
No fairy takes.
Nor witch hath power to charm.

So hallow'd and so gracious is the time.

—William Shakespeare

*For unto us a child is born, unto us a son is given:
and the government shall be upon his shoulder: and his
name shall be called Wonderful, Counsellor, The mighty
God, The everlasting Father, The Prince of Peace. Of the
increase of his government and peace there shall be no end,
upon the throne of David, and upon his kingdom,
to order it, and to establish it with judgment and
with justice from henceforth even for ever.*

ISAIAH 9:6-7 KJV

Jesus

Wonderful—He would be wonderful in what He would accomplish for the fallen human race.

Counselor—He would be our Guide through life, and our Advocate before the heavenly Father.

The Mighty God—He would be the God before whom every knee shall one day bow.

The Everlasting Father—He would be the God of eternity.

The Prince of Peace—He would be the One who would ultimately bring a true tranquillity among all nations.

—Kenneth W. Osbeck

The very purpose of Christ's coming into the world was that He might offer up His life as a sacrifice for the sins of men. He came to die. This is the heart of Christmas.

—Rev. Billy Graham

A Christmas Blessing

God grant you the light in Christmas, which is faith; the warmth of Christmas, which is love; the radiance of Christmas, which is purity; the righteousness of Christmas, which is justice; the belief in Christmas, which is truth; the all of Christmas, which is Christ.

—Wilda English

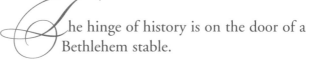

The hinge of history is on the door of a
Bethlehem stable.

—Ralph W. Sockman

*The shepherds . . . went with haste
and found Mary and Joseph, and
the child lying in the manger.*

LUKE 2:15-16 NRSV

If . . . we open our hearts and embrace Him . . . not only to reap abundance and joy and health and happy fulfillment, but also for the cancellation of our sins—then this is the greatest welcome we can give to the Christ child.

—Norman Vincent Peale

A personal Jesus accepted means salvation; a personal Jesus obeyed is sanctification; a personal Jesus followed is a life of brotherly kindness and true philanthropy; a personal Jesus reigning in the heart is the fullness of peace and joy and power. The bells of Bethlehem ring one note; the Christmas carols are all calling aloud the same note: "Back to Christ! Back to Christ!"

—T. L. Cuyler

Since you have been chosen by God who has given you this new kind of life . . . you should practice tenderhearted mercy and kindness to others.

COLOSSIANS 3:12 TLB

"Ready for Christmas," she said with a sigh
As she gave a last touch to the gifts piled high . . .
Then wearily sat for a moment to read
Till soon, very soon, she was nodding her head.
Then quietly spoke a voice in her dream,
"Ready for Christmas, what do you mean?"
She woke with a start and cry of despair.
"There's so little time and I've still to prepare.
Oh Father! Forgive me, I see what You mean!
To be ready means more than a house swept clean.
Yes, more than the giving of gifts and a tree.
A heart that is free from bitterness and sin.
So be ready for Christmas—and ready for Him!"

—Unknown

No warm, downy pillow His sweet head pressed;

No soft garments His fair form dressed;

He lay in a manger, this Heavenly Stranger,

The precious Lord Jesus, the wonderful Child.

—Unknown

There are some of us who think to ourselves,
"If I had only been there!
How quick I would have been to help the Baby.
I would have washed His linen.
How happy I would have been
to go with the shepherds
to see the Lord lying in the manger!"

We say that because we know how great Christ is.
But if we had been there at that time,
we would have done no better
than the people of Bethlehem.

We have Christ in our neighbor.
Why not serve Him now!

—Martin Luther

his Jesus of Nazareth, without money and arms, conquered more millions than Alexander, Caesar, Mohammed, and Napoleon.

—Phillip Schaff

Do not be afraid; for see—I am bringing you good news of great joy for all the people.

LUKE 2:10 NRSV

He was born in an obscure village, the child of a peasant woman. He grew up in another obscure village where He worked in a carpentry shop until He was thirty. Then for three years He was an itinerant preacher.

He never had a family or owned a home. He never set foot inside a big city. He never traveled two hundred miles from the place He was born. He never wrote a book or held an office. He did none of the things that usually accompany greatness.

Twenty centuries have come and gone, and today He is the central figure for much of the human race. All the armies that ever marched and all of the navies that ever sailed and all the parliaments that ever sat and all the kings that ever reigned, put together, have not affected the lives of man upon this earth as powerfully as this . . .

One Solitary Life.

Endnotes

1 *Ranger Rick,* December 1997.

2 "Heart to Heart, Everyday Glimpses of Humor and Hope," *Today's Christian Woman* (Nov./Dec. 1994).

3 Used by permission of Sword of the Lord Publishers, an imprint of Sword of the Lord Publishers.

4 *Illustrations Unlimited,* James Hewett (Wheaton, Ill: Tyndale House), 1988.

5 *The Work of Christmas,* Howard Thurman.

6 *The Speaker's Sourcebook,* Glenn Van Ekeren (Prentice Hall), 1988.

7 *Open the Door* (Charles Scribner's Sons), 1949.

8 *The Tenth Century,* December 1997.

Additional copies of this book and other Christmas titles
are available from your local bookstore.

A Treasury of Christmas Joy
The Wonder of Christmas
Merry Christmas
God's Little Christmas Book
Everything I Need to Know about Christmas I Learned from Jesus
Christmas Treasures of the Heart
The Greatest Christmas Ever
The Christmas Cookie Cookbook
The Candymaker's Gift
The Living Nativity